STORIES FROM THE SHELTER

FROM ST. FRANCIS CENTER—DENVER COLORADO

DR. PHILLIP K. TOMPKINS

outskirts press

Outskirts Press, Inc.
http://www.outskirtspress.com

ISBN: 978-1-9772-2396-8

Outskirts Press and the "OP" logo are trademarks belonging to Outskirts Press, Inc.

PRINTED IN THE UNITED STATES OF AMERICA

Stories from the Shelter
Table of Contents

Introduction

Guests of shelters for homeless persons are often seen as anonymous individuals, with troubled pasts and problematic futures. They are even seen as "nuisances" in many circumstances.

Yet, each has a story…. stories about how they got there, how they are living and surviving, where they are going; stories about hidden knowledge and talents; stories about problems and incidents; stories about successes and tragedies. Far from being anonymous, shelter guests are people that surprise, endear, frustrate, amuse, amaze, challenge, teach — and much more.

This book has stories collected by Dr. Phillip K. Tompkins from guests, volunteers, and staff of St. Francis Center, a non-profit day shelter in Denver, Colorado. St. Francis Center was founded in 1983 to provide day shelter from the weather for homeless persons. Over time its services have expanded to include some meals; showers; laundry; clothing; mail services; notary; phone charging; personal effects storage; counseling and social services navigation; employment services including for ex-felons; personal hygiene services. St. Francis Center also owns and operates facilities with transitional housing for guests who are ready. However, often St. Francis Center is simply a place to be. It was opened in a part of town that might have been called a "skid row" and now is in an area in transition to gentrification. It is part of Denver's tapestry of government and nonprofit services, working with other nonprofits to help individuals who are homeless make the transition to a better place in life.

St Francis Center opens at 6:10 am and closes at 5:30 pm as guests then seek a shelter that provides overnight stays. Or some guests simply look for a place to "camp out" for the night. Every day, on average, approximately 800 men and women come to St. Francis Center's shelter seeking emergency assistance during daytime hours. Its website is www.sfcdenver.org.

The purpose of this book is to share some of the many stories of St. Francis Center guests, volunteers and staff. We believe you will find these stories inspiring, funny, tragic, depressing, informative.

More than anything, we hope this book will help bring the homeless women and men into focus as real people with these real stories.

It may even inspire some readers to help improve the future stories of Denver's homeless by joining the ranks of volunteers. *Note: The author of each story acknowledged at the end of the story.*

To see each person

There are many lenses through which to view the day shelter which is St. Francis Center. There are the lenses of the Director, the Board, the donor, the volunteer, and that of the Staff, whether working in Basic Services, Administration or Outreach. There are the lenses of the person newly-homeless, disoriented and frightened, haltingly answering questions at the Intake Desk and the guest-who-is-almost-a-resident, who checks in by greeting the staff by name, checks her mail, signs up for a shower, hopes she gets a chair in her favorite section, and gets in line for a chore so she can shop later in the Clothing Room. Then there are the unique lenses of a potential volunteer taking a tour; the firemen called for a guest who has collapsed; the massage therapist who occasionally donates his services. The lens through which I see when I look at St. Francis Center is that of a retired social worker eager to do something to ease the lives of her neighbors without homes who has found a place of service which both uses my abilities and honors my limitations.

I volunteer two partial days a week at St. Francis Center. On Wednesdays I work in Office 6, the Social Services Office, assisting guests in filling out housing applications. It may not sound very tempting but I learned long ago as a social worker the power of a form accurately completed and also, the value of face-to-face conversation with a client, or guest as they are known at St. Francis Center. Our guests are by definition in distress. Finding themselves without a roof over their heads is usually just the most recent of a series of unfortunate events. If I can make enough of a human connection to get accurate information, perhaps St. Francis Center can be one of a series of helpful encounters which might lead to stability. I work half-days because I live with limitations due to chronic fatigue.

St. Francis Center exists because of its volunteer staff of just about three hundred. Given the continuous need for volunteers, the process could be expected to be rather rigid. Of course, certain slots must be filled for daily operations to proceed, but I know they were not looking to recruit a retired social worker with an interest in housing and not too much energy on the day I showed up. I sensed here that I was seen as I was and accepted for what I had to offer. I sensed that tone in the larger space as I was shown around. Now several years later, I am quite sure that "seeing each person" is deep in the heart of the institution. I see it routinely as I move around the shelter.

When a guest comes to Office 6 with a need, they sign up on a list hanging by the door. There are several Case Managers available and names are called in order, then crossed off after the guest leaves. Periodically a guest asks, or demands to know, how long the wait will be. The answer is always the same. "We don't know because we don't know what people need until we talk to them. If you can't wait, come back tomorrow." That sounded rigid to me at first. In time I realized that clear procedures are a gift to our guests. They live with a lot of chaos, things seem to happen to them randomly. Our apparent rigidity, assures order and also, that each person will get undivided attention in turn.

Of course, the order we try to preserve is sometimes not a match for the chaos within some of our guests. Office 6 is a moderate size room with three large desks, one small computer desk, a copier, a stack of file cabinets and two doors. Most of the time the four of us at the four desks are talking with a guest each, which makes for a rather crowded space. We work hard at focusing on the one person we are assisting, but we cannot help but overhear other speakers.

I remember the first time I overheard a guest express his frustration in a rising voice and increasingly irate language. I waited for some kind of an intervention, but I heard nothing. In a few minutes, the guest gathered his stuff and still mumbling, walked out. I heard nothing from the Staff Person, but she was in my line of vision and as I continued with the guest in front of me, I saw her sit very still, eyes focused on the face of the angry guest, not arguing, just listening. She could not offer what he was demanding, but she could – and did – give him her attention. The guest had gone too far in his anger to be able to acknowledge it, but he did leave and the business of the office continued.

When I'm not with a guest, I try to keep the housing applications up-to-date. One day my concentration was broken by a rough question, "Could I get a little help here? What's the matter with you guys? " I often sit at the computer desk, which is only a few feet from the door, so I was a bit alarmed – until I looked up and saw the grin on the face of the speaker. I glanced at Midori, one of the Case Managers, just as she snapped back, "Well, look who's here. Are you crabby today? If so, don't even think you can talk to me!" They both laughed and Midori continued, "Reach over. Don't you ever learn?" And the guest entered as if he'd been given the most gracious invitation.

Story from Pam Hubbard, St. Francis Center volunteer

"I don't want to be homeless"

I stepped out of Office 6 to walk over to the lounge to do some scanning when I heard a woman wailing, "No, no, no! I don't want to be homeless! I just want to work, but no one will hire me if I stink!"

Of course, staff tended to her with swiftness and gentleness and calm returned. One of our male guests caught my eye and said, "Sorry for the drama. Thanks for volunteering." I smiled and moved on. I was so affected I couldn't respond in the moment, but I thought of her cry and thought, it is my cry on their behalf whatever their story, whatever the reason. We can't survive if we live at that level of emotional rawness, but may we never forget it either. We are in this together.

Story from Pam Hubbard, St. Francis Center volunteer

A conversation in the shower

It was two or three minutes before 8:00 a.m. on Friday morning,

March 29, when I unlocked the door to the workspace behind the V-shaped counters in the Men's Showers. There waiting for me were fifteen or twenty men who had entered through another door to the larger room with toilets, dressing benches, sinks, mirrors and the showers.

"Could I have a towel?" asked several of them.

I brought in the baskets of bath towels, hand towels, and wash rags to put on the shelves under the counters before handing them out. Then I got some standard items to put on the point where the two counters met: Q-tips, mouthwash, lotion, plastic cups, while trying to keep up with the requests for soap, "smellgood" (aftershave and cologne), razors, tooth-brushes, and other items. Before long the baskets in the dressing area were full of used towels that I had to carry, with plastic gloves, back to the laundry, pausing there to get a clean basket of towels to take back.

A handsome, muscular man naked from the waist up came to the counter to finish dressing and talk. He got my attention and began to talk about his father. He said his father was not a good man, but then he tapped on the top of his forehead and said

"They did surgery here several times for brain cancer but he didn't complain when it was time to go."

After a pause he asked

"What did you do before this job?"

"I was a Professor of Communication and Comparative Literature."

Several men looked at me as I turned to assay the dressing and shower areas.

"Did, did, did you say you like literacy?" said a man with a stammer.

"Literature," I answered.

"Do, do, do you know Threw?"

I did not understand.

"Maybe he means Thoreau," said another man. The stammering man nodded.

"And Ralph Waldo. . . ," said a different man.

"Emerson," I said to complete his question," and "Yes, I taught Thoreau's work in some classes."

A tall black man moved up to the counter and asked

"Did you know he went to jail?"

"Yes," I answered, "and do you remember *why* he went to jail?"

He shook his head. No one else answered.

"He went to jail because he did not pay his taxes. He was opposed to the War in Mexico and the Fugitive Slave Law. It said if a slave got into a free state he had to be returned to his owner. Thoreau refused to do that, putting the escaped slaves up at his place."

"Wow," said the black man. He and others were a bit excited.

"Do you know what he wrote in jail?" I had unconsciously slipped back into the classroom, to the question and answer method.

"No," said several men.

"He wrote an essay, 'On Civil Disobedience,' in which he said that if you disagreed with laws passed by the government you had the moral right to disobey—in a peaceful way."

The several men liked those ideas, smiling and nodding.

"And a man working in Africa read 'On Civil Disobedience' and went back to India to lead a peaceful campaign of disobedience to the country that had colonized them, Great Britain."

I now had a small class of students at both counters giving me their rapt attention.

"And when a young black man in the United States read about Gandhi and Thoreau he started his own movement, a nonviolent campaign for civil rights. His name was Martin Luther King, Jr."

Several men began talking, many of them smiling.

"I was at his lake when I was a kid," said an older white man.

"Do you mean Walden Pond? I visited it also, the place where Thoreau built a cabin and wrote the book about his experience there. Did you live in Massachusetts?"

"Yes," he said with a big smile that showed he was missing the front tooth on his right side., and gave me the name of a town that I didn't quite catch. Then he grinned again as he said

"We should do some *more* reading."

Story from Dr. Phillip K. Tompkins, St. Francis Center volunteer

"Somebody took my pants!"

I worked yesterday at the shelter, one hour in the clothing room, two hours in the men's showers. The latter is the toughest job in the shelter because a basket full of wet towels is heavy. I have to tote them back to an industrial sized laundry. While in the showers, two men told me separately that they were going over to Coors Field to work the opening day game between the Rockies and the Dodgers. One was going to serve refreshments, the other said he would park cars.

As I was finishing up at 11:00 a man came up to the counter and said, "I am sorry but is there anything you can do for me? While I was taking a shower somebody took my pants."

I thought about getting a pair in the clothing room so I asked him about size: "34 x 34" he answered sadly. As I started to leave an idea came to me: "Did you have a wallet in your pants."

"Oh, my God, my car keys, wallet and ID," as he hurried back to the dressing area.

I walked up front to find the Coordinator for the day, but she had just gone into a meeting. I told the man filling in for her and he ran back to the showers. From there I went to the lunch room where three friends were having a bite. I told them about it and they became sad with me. We try to make the quality of life better for our guests and something like this loss hurts us all.

I said my goodbyes to my friends and headed for the door. The man filling in was sitting in the greeter's spot.

"What did you do for the man?"

"Oh, he found the pants. They were under his shirt," he said with a smile.

I turned and walked rapidly to the lunch room to tell my friends the good news. They were greatly relieved.

Story from Dr. Phillip K. Tompkins, St. Francis Center volunteer

"I'm self-conscious about this"

I had noticed that in the past Frank, from Trinity United Methodist Church, ate his lunch at the smaller table. I tried a couple of times to get him to join the others at the bigger table. I asked him again today and he said:

"I'm self-conscious about this," pointing to his walker.

I shook my head and pointed to the chair next to me. He came over. And then took off his cap for the first time, revealing his baldness.

We got into a conversation and he mentioned a time in the past and referred to his "fiancé."

"Did you get married?" I asked.

He nodded and added, "I am a widower."

I sympathized.

"See you next week."

Story from Dr. Phillip K. Tompkins, St. Francis Center volunteer

A poem

It was on Friday, during my shift from 8:00 a.m. to 9:00, when I had a conversation with several men in the shower room. A man asked me what I did before volunteering at the shelter and I answered that I had been a Professor of Communication and Comparative Literature. Then came questions and comments about Henry David Thoreau. From there I moved a few feet to work the 9:00 a.m. shift behind the counter in the Clothing Room. I was working with a fellow volunteer from Trinity United Methodist Church, named Frank.

The numbers were being passed out to determine the order in which our homeless guests would enter the Clothing Room so Frank and I had a moment to chat. He reminded me that I had given him a copy of my 2009 book, *Who is My Neighbor?: Communicating and Organizing to End Homelessness.*

"I have read the book once and am reading it again a second time," said Frank. "Do you remember the section where you talk about the *Voice*, the homeless newspaper?"

"Yes, but you don't see it much anymore," I said.

"You talk about the poems in the newspaper and I wrote one that was published in it."

I was stunned. I had heard no hint that Frank was a writer, a poet. He handed me a single sheet of white paper that I began to read. It is included on the next page so you will see it in the same form Frank presented it to me.

Thirty Dollars

My home. Behind dumpster.
Live there. Sleep with gravel
        tearing my cheekbone.
Get work sometimes –
        not enough paycheck
        to move out.
Food, cigs, quart of beer,
Money spent.

Need to use facility.
Some businesses just say "no."
Others have restrooms that read:
        "Customers Only."
But money spent.

Go back home. Behind dumpster.
Doin' my business.

White car pulls up.
Officer steps out:
"Urinating in public."

Fifteen dollar fine.
Fifteen dollar court costs.
Thirty dollars
        for pissing
        on my own home. . .

poem by Frank Russell
from The Denver Voice
January 2000

I was moved. I looked at Frank, then back at the poem. I was moved even more and each time I read it silently or out loud. Then I saw something new. In typing it today, I noticed the ironic meaning in saying that he had not enough paycheck to "move out," as if he could get inside and outside his spot on the ground behind the dumpster, and as if he could piss "on" his house.

We were busy with men seeking the right size of blue jeans, underwear, socks, and tee shirts. A few women shopped with us for themselves and for their man. But we kept up an oral conversation of short sentences, like the old telegraphs for which you paid by the word. Frank did acknowledge that he was homeless for a while.

"How long?"

"About three months."

"Why?"

"It was my fault. But I did not have friends with enough resources to help me out."

He knew I would understand what he met. In the homeless book I talk about "social capital" and communication links that can help people. When talking to an audience or in conversation I would come up with a line like this:

"I daresay that if you fell on hard times you would have friends and family members who would put you up for a while, help you with rent and other ways." I always seem to get nods of agreement. But having read the book after being homeless, Frank was telling me he did not have the generous communication links or social capital to help him stay "out" of his home behind the dumpster.

Frank has given me permission to share with others. Frank has not only been an outstanding colleague as a volunteer, we now know part of his source of empathy and compassion. In volunteering at St. Francis Center, I never thought I would stand beside such a man helping others find the right "fit" in life.

Story from Dr. Phillip K. Tompkins, St. Francis Center volunteer

A toothbrush

I love the interactions I'm having at St Francis Center. Last week a young woman, no more than 22 or so, asked for toothpaste. She didn't have a toothbrush, she was going to put it on her finger. I asked if she wanted a toothbrush -- but she didn't have the 10 cents for it. I gave it to her anyway -- and I put my 10 cents in the drawer.

Story from Margaret Prentice, St. Francis Center volunteer

"Happy Good Friday!"

It was a wonderful Friday at the St. Francis Center. As I checked in a few minutes before my 8:00 shift in the men's showers I saw a staff member who greeted me with

"Happy Good Friday!"

I carried that with me into the showers. The general attitude was rather neutral so I began to repeat the greeting I had received.

"Ok," said a man at the counter, "but how can it be a good day if someone got killed?"

I remembered that as a child I was baffled by that same question. I got a new perspective on it recently while watching a show on Netflix about Jesus. Some thinkers and writers now label Judas as heroic for identifying Jesus. Otherwise there may not have been a crucifixion and resurrection. So I kept wishing guests a "Happy Good Friday!" A white man asked

"Could I have a toothbrush?"

"Ten cents," was my standard reply.

"Oh, I don't have ten cents" the man said sadly.

When I turned back from the toothbrush shelf I saw a tall black man counting out pennies on the counter, five in one stack and then five more in another. I handed the other man a toothbrush and scooped up the ten pennies while the black man produced a smile. Everyone grinned and someone said

"Good Friday!"

Don't tell the boss, but I later gave a toothbrush to a man who had only five cents. And another to a man who was broke.

When I got home there was an email announcing that my granddaughter Vanessa had given birth to a baby boy, Timothy, both in good health, and making me a great grandfather for the first time.

Happy Good Friday indeed...

Story from Dr. Phillip K. Tompkins, St. Francis Center volunteer

An alumni gift

When I took a short break at 10:00 in our lunch room I saw a couple of staff members scooping ice cream into bowls. I turned to Susan, a staff member and asked what was happening.

"A former guest sent us $1,000 to "do something nice for our current guests."

I was moved. A former guest who must appreciate what we did to help him or her get ahead in life wanted to do "something nice" for today's guests. It also reminded me that something like eighty percent of our guests disappear after about thirty days or so.

Story from Dr. Phillip K. Tompkins, St. Francis Center volunteer

"The Empire of Anguish"

As I walked toward the door to the showers on a busy but quiet day, a few minutes before 8:00 a.m. a guest named Joe stopped me. He began talking about the police in ways that were difficult to comprehend. But in retrospect he was telling me so that I could help him understand why the Denver police told a woman in her sixties he knows that "she was going to be killed." Perhaps he read the lack of understanding on my face because he switched topics. Or did he?

"The Gallup polls indicate that Americans are the most stressed people in the world."

"Yes," I answered, "I heard Lester Holt on NBC news last night say that polls indicated the same thing."

"I have created a phrase for it," continued Joe, I call us the Empire of Anguish."

Story from Dr. Phillip Tompkins, St. Francis Center volunteer

"No smellgood"

It was a busy but quiet morning. Men talked about the weather, how nice it was and how warm it would get later in the day. They seemed eager to get cleaned up and get back out in the open. For the second Friday we were not handing out bars or pieces of soap to the guests. I showed them the large plastic container full of a green body wash and the small plastic cups to fill wand take to the sink or showers. Staff members told me there was an epidemic of some kind that might be passed by two people using the same piece of soap. They were not sure what kind of infection we feared.

"Could I have some smellgood, some aftershave?"

"No aftershave and the only cologne we have is, say other guests, for women."

Most men waved it away but some did spray it on bare skin and shirts and jackets. Then someone took the bottle with him.

"No smellgood?" was the response I got after that.

The highlight of serving as the bartender behind the counter was a conversation with a late middle-aged guest. As he turned to leave the room he raised a hand to his head and said

"Thank you, my friend."

Story from Dr. Phillip K. Tompkins, St. Francis Center volunteer

"I'm gonna be rich"

After I took charge of the Men's Shower, an old, slender, white haired man walking with a limp and a cane held in a bandaged arm slowly moved toward the exit.

"How is it going?"

"I have a broken arm and foot but I'm gonna be rich," he said with a broad smile.

"Why? How?"

"Bacchus and Schanker have taken my case!"

I recognized the name of the law firm from their television ads claiming they can help people hurt in automobile accidents. He said a woman looked one way but not the other as she turned to run over him.

"Good luck," I gave as a farewell.

Story from Dr. Phillip K. Tompkins, St. Francis Center volunteer

Cultural Norms

A tall white man walked into the area of the sinks and looked in the mirror. He turned his head from side to side and brushed his dark hair with his hand, saying

"If I'm going to be homeless I should look like a bum."

When he finished telling me this a short, dark man with long black hair walked up to the counter about eight feet away from us and placed a small object on the counter, saying

"Somebody left this."

I walked the distance to see what it was. I picked up a coin, a U.S. 25 cent piece, a quarter. As I put it in its proper place in the cabinet behind me the thought came: *One would think that "Finder's Keepers" would be the cultural norm in a homeless shelter.*

Cultural Norms. Guests at St. Francis Center have all kinds, just like the larger social system.

Story from Dr. Phillip K. Tompkins, St. Francis Center volunteer

Mothers Day

When I arrived to relieve the man who worked the showers from 7:00 to 8:00 he said things had gone well. He added that he reminded the men that Sunday is Mother's Day. That got filed into my memory bank as I scanned the large area from toilets to sinks to dressing area to showers. Things were in order.

One of the 8:00 a.m. regulars in the showers is a tall, handsome man with light skin and African features. He asked for the towels and toiletries he needed. As he was walking toward the showers I the memory surfaced and I said

"Happy Mother's Day."

He stopped, tuned to me and said "My Little sister."

"What?"

"My sister in now my mother."

Of the five men I gave such a wish as they left, two of them surprised me by saying "my sister is now my mother."

There is a man who often takes up to an hour to wash, rinse, and comb his hair in a sink, naked from the waist up and a towel covering his front from the waist down. He walked up to the counter and said softly

"I was on an elevator when a man got on and said 'be quiet, my mother died.'"

Story from Dr. Phillip K. Tompkins, St. Francis Center volunteer

Pennies

At ten o'clock I went into the showers. It was fairly busy, what with requests for towels, wash cloths, and a towel to stand on. And for "smellgood," one word for either aftershave or cologne. Razors are ten cents apiece, tooth brushes also a dime, and combs and "picks" are for sale at a nickel apiece.

Several guests paid for their item by pennies. Then a man bought three razors for thirty pennies. Another bought a comb and tooth brush for fifteen pennies. I got to the point where I stopped counting the pennies if the group looked large enough. Another guest gave me twenty five pennies for his items.

Later I reflected on the Abrahamic Affluence of our guests. It came back to me from years ago when a man cashed in fifty pennies for a two quarters. I asked him where he got them all. He showed me an even larger bag of them. Then he went on to say that when he walked the streets of downtown Denver he looked in the gutter around parking meters. Often there will be a bunch of pennies, presumably dropped there by citizens who were members of the Washingtonian Affluence. While impatiently searching pockets and purses for quarters to feed the meter they dumped the worthless pennies in the gutter. There is my observation of the day: How fortunate we are that our homeless citizens help clean up the streets of our city.

Story from Dr. Phillip K. Tompkins, St. Francis Center volunteer

Underwear --your choice

I moved on to the Clothing Room at 9:00 to work with two other volunteers; Frank the Poet behind the counters and Nurse Pat at the door letting people in who had earned a clothing slip by hard work.

Despite using a walker, whenever a guest asks for underwear, Frank asks what size and then picks up the entire large basket of underwear, letting the guest pick from briefs, or "tighty whiteys," boxers, or boxer briefs. After working behind the counter for over twenty years, only recently did I begin picking up the proper box of underwear or socks—boxed by gender and color—and hoist it onto the counter so the guest can make a selection.

Story from Dr. Phillip K. Tompkins, St. Francis Center volunteer

The Belt

A bright, sunny day it was when I arrived at the homeless shelter, St. Francis Center, at 7:45 on a Friday morning. I got some hot water for my travelling tea container and relieved a faithful volunteer named James in the Men's Showers at 8:00. It was one of the quietest mornings ever, so much so that I began to count the number of men, about 20, using our sinks, toilets, and showers. Then a tall, handsome man with a great smile walked up to my counter:

"May I offer you this as a donation?" he asked while holding up a sturdy leather belt.

"Sure, I can hang it on one of the empty nails in the clothing room."

I had no one waiting to request anything so I went out my back door into the Clothing Room and hung it on a nail, giving us a total of one belt in stock. Not long after I did it I saw that same smiling face.

"Do you still have that belt I gave you?"

"Yes, it is hanging own a nail in the Clothing Room."

"Could I have it back?"

Disappointed, I nodded and again went out my back door to retrieve the belt. When I handed it back he still had the smile and said:

"I found a guy with a need for it."

Story from Dr. Phillip K. Tompkins, St. Francis Center volunteer

Shower by Appointment

Business picked up as I carried the dirty towels through my back door to the Laundry, bringing back clean towels, floor mats, and wash rags. I had plenty of "smellgood," aftershave and cologne, warning the men that the some women couldn't resist the stuff. There was an old, rather feeble white man waiting at the counter nearest the door. He asked for three towels, soap, and shampoo. He gathered them up and turned toward the door.

"Wait," I said, "you can't take them out of the showers," pointing toward the sign on the wall with that message.

"I've got an appointment at the shower up front at 8:30."

"You mean the women's showers?"

"No," he answered impatiently, slowly walking toward the door.

What was that all about? I asked myself. *I will have to ask about this incident; I hope I did not break the rules.*

When I finished at 9:00 I worked in the Clothing Room with Pat at the door accepting the earned clothing slips from the guests in line. Frank the Poet worked with me behind the counter in the area containing men's pants, underwear, tee shirts, and socks. I kept wondering about letting the man go with the three clean towels, hoping I had not broken the rule.

Another hour in the laundry was spent with worry as I rolled many, many new white socks for the Clothing Room. I believe it was Joan the nurse who said there was a new shower stall at the front of the center.

But then Crystal, our Volunteer Coordinator, came into the lunch room and told me that I did not need to bring anything to the workshop on Wednesday dealing with the effects of trauma. She was pleased I had signed up for it. I asked her about the man with the towels.

"Yes," she said, "you did the right thing. There is a shower with a seat for people who have a legitimate reason for taking a shower without anyone seeing them. They make appointments to take it."

"Could it be that lesbians, gay men and transgender persons might use it?"

"Yes."

Andrew Spinks, our number two administrator, joined our conversation and mentioned "those guys who may have had an accident and do not want to look like a fool while undressing in the big showers."

"And if the smaller Women's Showers get too crowded, a female guest can sign up for an appointment for the other shower," said Crystal.

I nodded, getting a natural high—ekstasis—because once again the St. Francis Center proved to be sensitive to the needs of our guests. Perhaps St. Francis himself might applaud the new facility and rule.

Andrew and Crystal then talked to each other about organizational communication, one of my research and teaching subjects as a practicing professor, agreeing that they should think through who should be informed about the new facility—about a month old—said Andrew. I nodded, satisfied that my instincts were correct and that we are now doing even more to give our guests a few more degrees of Being.

Story from Dr. Phillip K. Tompkins, St. Francis Center volunteer

Communication -- or not

Andrew and Crystal could not have known that my doctoral degree was granted to me in 1962 by Purdue University in a new field now called Organizational Communication. I was one of the first recipients of a Ph.D. degree in this new field. One of the best ways I can explain the new field is to explain the work of a pioneering organizational expert, Chester I. Barnard.

Barnard was a successful and thoughtful business manager who gave lectures about his work and then wrote a classic book published by the Harvard University Press in 1938: *The Functions of the Executive.* In it he wrote that there are three elements of organization: 1) communication; 2) willingness to serve; and 3) common purpose. It turns out that all three have serious communication implications.

The first element is now obvious; organization is not possible without communication—e.g., orders and feedback. The willingness to serve must be created by executives, that is, managers who will recruit, will persuade people to accept a position within the organization and continue to serve. The St. Francis Center is constantly recruiting people to maintain a crew of 200 volunteers. Common purpose can come about only if the executive *articulates a purpose* that others are willing to serve.

As an early student of organizational communication I was the first to summarize existing research on the subject at a conference sponsored by NASA. I was also a Summer

Faculty Consultant in 1967 and 1968 to Dr. Wernher von Braun, Director of NASA's Marshall Space Flight Center during the development of the Saturn V, the rocket that took the first man to the Moon. I have written articles about the brilliant communication practices Dr. von Braun developed for NASA, and how they contributed to the success of the Apollo Project. I have also sadly written two books about the failures of two Space Shuttles, Challenger and Columbia, because of failures in organizational communication.

Pardon this academic footnote, but notice how my ignorance of the new shower made me reluctant to serve the customer. Andrew and Crystal recognized that my doubt and confusion meant that organizational communication had to be introduced in which all volunteers and staff members working in the Men's Showers had to know when to let guests take towels out of the room. The staff coordinators had to be informed so that they could in turn inform staff, volunteers and members about the new shower and what changes we would have to make in order to achieve our common purpose. I give Crystal and Andrew high marks for noticing the need to engage in formal organizational communication.

Story from Dr. Phillip K. Tompkins, St. Francis Center volunteer

Trauma and Mail

On Wednesday I joined about 50 other people meeting for four and a half hours in a workshop sponsored for the volunteers and staff members of St. Francis Center. There were volunteers from other shelters as well. The topic was trauma. I assumed the content would be pitched to help those who served people with traumas, but it became clear that it was also aimed at us, about handling our own.

The audience enjoyed the speaker, a fluent and funny self-identified Jew who later told us he suffered from the Holocaust Trauma. He said he and his Jewish friends had visas so as to be ready to run when it was about to come again, this time to the U.S. As a Professor Emeritus of Communication I agreed with much of what he said about trying to connect with trauma victims by a non-evaluative approach. "Tell me more, I am interested in what you are saying, listening carefully." At times people will gain insights into their own tendencies toward, say, "fight or flight" while explaining their traumas to a patient, nonjudgmental listener.

The eight people at our table were assigned by the lecturer to apply the teachings to the chore of helping our guests find their mail. Homeless people, by definition, have neither a mailing address nor a mailbox. One of our most important services is to give our guests a card with the shelter's mailing address so they can have a place to receive mail.

As I pointed out in our table's discussion, it is tough to apply the day's teachings about making a connection with homeless guests when there is a long line of other homeless guests waiting to have their mail checked. We did talk, however, about helping people who were disappointed about not getting a welfare check or a Driver's License in the mail.

Today at the shelter I heard other volunteers talk about how much they enjoyed the workshop. I was able to tell them that on Thursday I spent much of the morning reviewing my boyhood traumas, gaining some surprising insights.

Story from Dr. Phillip K. Tompkins, St. Francis Center volunteer

Why we do this

After I finished my work at 11:00 I met with friends at the lunch table. Crystal, our Volunteer Coordinator, sat down next to me with a white board and had me explain why I volunteered at the St. Francis Center in one sentence. I came up with this:

"Because I identify completely with the goals and services offered by the St. Francis Center." She wrote that in black ink on the white board for me to hold under my chin as she took my picture. Then she wanted me to expand on my reasons for volunteering.

I told her that after writing a book about homelessness and the St. Francis Center—*Who is My Neighbor?*—that was published in 2009, I heard from a Professor of Communication and Social Psychology at the University of California at Santa Barbara. His name is Howard Giles. He sent me a paper that summarizes the social scientific research on people who volunteer at organizations like SFC. I now quote from a later book of mine published by the Purdue University Press in 2015: *Managing Risk and Complexity through Open Communication and Teamwork.* I quote from page 161:

> When compared to similar people who do not volunteer, those who do are happier, have greater self respect, talk about their volunteer work, are healthier and live longer.

That helps explain why we do it.

Story from Dr. Phillip K. Tompkins, St. Francis Center volunteer

A Boy and his Blankets:
a story from the shelter for the Season of Giving

Not all stories from the shelter come from the showers. Let me provide some background for readers to understand this seasonal letter. My wife Elaine and I live in Brooks Tower, eight blocks from the St. Francis Center. I used to walk to and from the shelter when I started volunteering in 1998. Now I drive. For some time Mike Gadbury, the Head Maintenance man at Brooks Towers, has helped me store donations for St. Francis Center. In addition to storing the donations, people in a 42 story building often forget about clothes in the laundry room, left in both washers and dryers. When the donations are too many for my little car, Mike and I put them in his big pickup truck and make the trip.

Several weeks ago Mike stopped me and said that his nine year old grandson had saved all of his blankets and wanted to give them to homeless people. We decided it would be impossible for him to hand them out personally but we could deliver them to our homeless guests who earned a clothing slip by doing a chore such as sweeping, mopping, cleaning toilets, and other important jobs. Blankets are made available in the Clothing Room when the temperature turns downward.

Mike wanted to give his grandson some credit so he asked if we could make a little poster to put up. Then somebody came up with a better idea:

Put his picture in Saint Francis Center's Facebook space. I appealed to Crystal Rains, Coordinator of Volunteers, who does other important odd jobs. She sent off the message and photograph.

I do not subscribe to Facebook but my fellow volunteer and friend Frank Lewis told me it had appeared in a nice presentation. Yesterday I saw Mike and when I started to ask him if he had seen . . . . , he interrupted me to say "Yes," he said rearing his head back, "his mother thinks it is very good, and so does the boy."

We are into the Season of Giving. We did celebrate a high order of giving in the case of the boy and his blankets.

A big thank you to this kind and civic minded young man, nine- year old Alonzo Gonzales III, who donated SEVEN bags of important items for the guests of St. Francis Center. His generosity will help a number of our guests especially during these cold, winter months. St. Francis Center operates a clothing room out of our day center that is stocked completely with donations and is accessed free of charge by our guests after they sign up for and complete a chore around our center. It is because of donations like these that we are able to provide this crucial service to our guests.

Here is the picture of Alonzo Gonzales III

Story from Dr. Phillip K. Tompkins, St. Francis Center Volunteer

"Set'em up, barkeep !!"

It is Friday, June 14, and my work slip orders me to the Men's Showers at 8:00. When I go in the back door I discover that the room is full of men but the cabinet with toiletries is locked and the shelves for the different towels are empty. I go back up to the front and borrow the key of our coordinator, Zach. The men, some twenty five of them, are looking for me to give them what they need. I hustle back to the laundry for clean towels, large bath towels, floor mats, and wash cloths. Some are showering and shaving but most of them are waiting to ask for something. A black man says with a smile,

"Set 'em up, barkeep."

"Sometimes I feel like a bartender back here," I said with a laugh.

Slowly my supply caught up with their demand. They were so patient waiting for towels, soap, shampoo, conditioner, cologne and after shave. The requests for spray cologne has gone up in recent years. We were out of it today but I had a bottle of blue and another of green after shave. Some accepted it as a substitute but many wanted cologne or nothing.

With the exception of one guest the men were patient and appreciative, thanking me on the way out and wishing me a good day. I felt a greater sense of communion when a black man said

"Thank you bro."

Story from Dr. Phillip K. Tompkins, St. Francis Center volunteer

Never Underestimate the power of a –

It was quiet when I relieved the volunteer named James in the showers at 8:00 a.m. He had carried dirty towels back to the laundry and brought clean, folded ones placed on the shelves under the counter for me to dispense. One man asked for two razors and paid in two stacks of pennies. Another man offered a Ziploc bag of coins for a dollar bill. *Hmm,* I thought, *they must have been looking for leavings around parking meters.*

Then I overheard part of one of the best conversations ever in the showers. Two men with their backs to me were shaving, looking in the mirror and then at each other as they talked. One asked

"Have you read . . . ." and I missed the title.

"Yes, I read it. I read it in prison. I read it in prison and it made me good. Now I am out of prison."

The other man asked if he had read another book, the title of which I also missed, by the same author. Oh, how I wish to know the name of the book that made the man good. We should not underestimate the power of a book.

Story from Dr. Phillip K. Tompkins, St. Francis Center volunteer

Feet and Socks

I would have asked them but I was concerned because of the shortages behind the counter: no mouthwash, no cologne, no clean socks. All are important but the socks are *crucial.* Homeless people are on their feet much more than those of us with a home and a car. You can sometimes see the concern as they take off shoes and socks for a shower. A next door neighbor of mine, a nurse named Jo, sometimes comes into the shelter to help people with bad feet. She washes them and then tends to their wounds.

The St. Francis Center decided many years ago to provide a service to men in the showers. They can get a pair of clean socks by dropping their dirty pair into a bucket under an opening in the counter.

The bucket has a disinfectant and when full we carry it back to the laundry for washing and recycling. Matching the washed socks for some volunteers is a frustrating exercise. But one volunteer named Margaret recently told me she is in a state of delight as she matches, goes beyond her assigned hours. She still wonders, however, how a pair washed together can have one clean and one dirty sock. So this morning I had a group of men with a pair of dirty socks in hand and a look of anticipation on the face. I alerted the volunteers in the laundry and they soon presented me with a basket of clean socks. That helped make my day in the showers, lifting the basket up on the counter so each could pick his favorite pair.

At nine I was replaced and moved behind another counter to work with Frank the Poet, this one in the Clothing Room. We help guests who have been checked by Pat, the volunteer at the door, for a work slip earned by doing a chore—sweeping, mopping, cleaning toilets. Frank and I help them find the right pants, tee shirts, underwear, and socks. Ah, socks again, but in this place they have earned new socks. Most homeless men select new white socks over those of color. Why? My best guess is that white socks most readily show grime and blood, time to tend to feet and get clean socks.

Story from Dr. Phillip K. Tompkins, St. Francis Center volunteer

A Shave and a Haircut....

This morning I got there at about 7:55 to relieve James in the showers.

"I thought maybe you stayed on the River Walk in San Antonio," said James with his broad smile that reveals the irony of his words. I had missed last Friday as I attended the wedding of my grandson in San Antonio.

It was good to be back. The men were polite and expressed thanks and appreciation for the service and toiletries, especially the "smellgood," and we had both aftershave and cologne. I was troubled by the young man in the stocking hat and overcoat who glances left, then right, and today murmured loud enough for me to hear him the first time.

A handsome Asian man bought a razor and asked for the towels for a shower and a shave. After his shower I saw him stand in front of a mirror and lather his head. Then he put the razor to work.

"How often do you shave your head?"

"About twice a month," he said after turning to his right to see me.

"Why do you do it?"

"Because I can't afford a haircut."

He smiled.

Story from Dr. Phillip K. Tompkins, St. Francis Center Volunteer

Black Friday

The clock/thermometer at 16th and Curtis said 20 degrees at 7:45am as I drove to the St. Francis Center on the Friday after Thanksgiving. I had been worrying for several days about our homeless guests out in the cold and snowy city. I checked in and relieved James at the Men's Showers just before 8:00, letting him move on to Mail and Storage. As I looked about the room I noticed a symptom of the numbing weather: even the men at the sinks who were washing, shaving, and brushing teeth still had their coats on. I had on three layers myself: including my red, black, and blue Pendleton jacket from the 1970s, saved for the Christmas period.

"Did you have a good meal yesterday?"

I put the question to a number of men.

"Yes, I ate several meals," said one man. His answer was typical, as they took advantage of Thanksgiving meals served at several times and places around the city of Denver. I walked the dirty towels back to the laundry, and carried clean ones back into the showers. While picking up some towels I heard loud voices coming from the other end of the room, the area where the urinals and toilet stalls are located. There were a half dozen men in coats looking into the toilet area. A tall man in front of a far toilet was shouting as loud as possible, using the "f" word. Yells from one of the urinals echoed his word choice. I started walking in that direction and shouted

"Stop it, quiet down!"

"[Expletive] you in your [expletive] red plaid Christmas jacket. He pulled a [expletive] knife on me!"

"Who did?"

Several men in the audience pointed to a man standing at a urinal with his back to me.

For me, this was a "déjà vu" moment…flashing back to another time when years ago when I was working behind the counter in the Men's Showers and a guest walked into the room through a door to the right of me.

He stopped, looked back at the door to see a man following him through the door and then raised his right arm and brought it down—in a flash of silver—on the man's head, then glancing off to his shoulder. The blood began to pour from above his ear.

As in the earlier situation, on this Black Friday I made a snap decision to bolt for help. This was dangerous and I could not let it go any further. I walked rapidly through the door to the Great Room and spotted our Coordinator for the day not far away.

"Zach!"

"What is it Phil?"

"One man claimed another pulled a knife on him."

We walked rapidly back through the door and Zach took charge. No doubt they recognized him as a staff member, with greater authority than I, and not wearing a Christmas Pendleton jacket. He got things under control and later told me that he thought somebody *threatened* to pull a knife. But did *not* actually pull it.

The group in the audience broke up and all the men went back to the showers and sinks. It did not seem like a normal Friday. Then came a voice over the loudspeaker calling staff to another altercation, this time in the Great Room. That usually meant tensions, name calling, or even violence. Later I learned that a fight broke out and the fighters were "86ed"—slang for "ejected."

I began to reflect on the day's two altercations so far. Could it be that the holiday season could be having a negative effect on our homeless guests? To the degree they had access to the media they had to know that this was Black Friday, the day we were all supposed to play the role of good citizens by participating in the biggest shopping day of the year. They were not good citizens while hanging out in a homeless shelter. It troubled me that this could be part of the unspoken atmosphere on Black Friday. "Black" in Black Friday meant businesses got out of the red on this day, but for our guests it might have its other, bleaker meaning.

I was relieved by a volunteer I did not know. He said he had never worked in the showers before so I stayed a bit to show him where things are kept. He caught on quickly.

At about 11:20 I went into the lunch room and met with volunteer friends, Joe, Pat, and Frank. I saw Zach sitting at the table eating a red pepper stuffed with other goodies. I got his attention.

"Zach, do you think the holidays could bother our guests?"

"Yes, I think it could bother some of them at least. They might remember a Thanksgiving or other holiday in the past when things were much better."

We were interrupted by the loud speaker calling for staff members to proceed to the great room. Zach and others left rapidly. I started another conversation with Joe, a volunteer and friend as he ate his lunch. When I left he wished that my car might start in the cold weather. On my way out I asked a young woman on staff serving as a greeter what had happened.

"A fight," she said.

"Fight?"

She nodded.

Story from Dr. Phillip K. Tompkins, St. Francis Center Volunteer

On a snowy day,
"Give me the rainbow."

It had snowed during the night and the flakes were still slightly falling when I woke up at 6:30. Snow should give pause to every volunteer and staff worker at a homeless shelter. Did the "soon to be guests at St Francis Center" get wet during the night? I drove the eight blocks and pulled into the parking lot with an inch or so on the ground.

I made it a bit before eight o'clock to get my work slip. Yes, off again to the showers. I went in to find about fifteen men wondering what to do without towels, soap, shampoo, and other items. I got set up and began to give them what they needed. The small number of men increased when the word got out that I had opened the shelves for all. I included offering a clean pair of socks in exchange for their dirty and perhaps damp pair.

It was quiet until a middle aged African American man with a bit of a beard and bald head began to give an oration to me. Actually it was more of a sermon, in the form of an interrogation. He lengthened the name "Phil" on my red volunteer name tag and began with:

"Phillllip, what would you do today if you went up to heaven?"

I shook my head as I kept listening to requests and passing out necessities.

"What would you say if today you met Jesus in heaven?"

I finally responded: "I don't know, I've never thought about it."

He continued: "What if you had been there for a long time and Jesus asked if you were ready for another life on Earth?"

I shook my head. As a student of the meaning of existence (existentialism), I feel one life is enough.

He went on in a kind of sing song way about heaven, concluding with the thought that Heaven has existed for eons compared to the shortness of time of life on Earth. He seemed to want me to say I would go for another life. When I failed to respond further, he moved on, perhaps to put these questions to others.

It became a good day in the showers when I brought in a basket full of dry socks on a snowy day. I was relieved at nine o'clock by Andy so that I could go back out the door and into the Clothing Room, working behind the counter for mainly men's garments with my friend Frank the Poet. We were pleased to see that someone in the hierarchy had decided at last to put out the long johns. It was time, a snowy day well into November with a temperature around freezing.

We were disappointed, even hurt, to learn that there were no pants in the waist size range from 30" to 36." Frank noticed it first and let out a sound of disappointment. Many homeless men are slender fellows, well we would be too if we did as much walking and not having a refrigerator full of snacks. A man about six feet tall with a hat and heavy hip-length coat on asked for a pair of stockings, then spotted a pair he liked.

"Oh, give me the rainbow," he asked.

My eye looked for a pair of socks and found one with bright colored rings around it. But it was in the wrong box.

"That's a women's pair of socks," I said to make sure he realized this fact.

"That is ok. I am one."

Story from Dr. Phillip K. Tompkins, St. Francis Center Volunteer

From Egypt to St. Francis Center

A tall white woman was talking to Frank about water, the effects of its availability and shortages. I jumped in:

"My wife and I recently watched a documentary about the Nile River on PBS. As they cross the driest part of the desert a camel fills up with water from the Nile. If I remember correctly, a camel can take in thirty gallons with a single gulp."

She seemed to agree and then said she had ridden a camel.

"Where?" I asked.

"In Egypt," she replied. "It is difficult to hang on when they get up from the ground." She imitated a camel getting up

"Because they bring their rear end up first and can throw you forward."

"What were you doing in Egypt?"

"Oh, we were on a honeymoon. I thought that instead of having a big wedding it would be more fun to travel through Egypt, Turkey, Greece and its islands."

Frank and I were astonished. What was she doing in here?

"But now we are divorced," she said with a forced smile.

"And I have six kids."

Story from Dr. Phillip K. Tompkins, St. Francis Center volunteer

Once a Boilermaker, always a Boilermaker

When I first volunteered at the St. Francis Center that year I walked to and from the shelter because it is only eight blocks away at 2323 Curtis. On Monday of this week I set out with a birthday card for my granddaughter to mail at the Post Office halfway on the route I used to walk to the shelter. When I crossed a busy 16th Street there were, as almost always, people waiting on Curtis for a bus.

"Phil?"

I looked to my right to see a tall, handsome African American man looking inquisitively at me.

"Yes."

"Purdue?"

"Yes, I am a Boilermaker," tapping my white baseball cap with an Old Gold and Black P above the brow.

We shook hands as I said "Boiler Up," and he laughed.

As I continued down Curtis I thought that there were two positive signs in that encounter: 1) I had not seen him at the shelter for a long time; and 2) He was no doubt waiting for a bus. I hoped it took him to a safe place.

Story from Dr. Phillip K. Tompkins, St. Francis Center volunteer

A Troubled Bridge over Healing Waters

My wife Elaine and I took Amtrak's California Zephyr to Glenwood Springs, Colorado. We walked up the stairs from the train station to enter the Denver Hotel across the street. We had Room 239 for two nights, enjoying the weather and the pool of hot springs. To get to the waters Native Americans considered sacred and possessing healing powers, we had to take an elevator up to a pedestrian bridge across the railroad tracks and the Colorado River and then climb down to the pools. On the afternoon of our arrival on Tuesday I was half way across the bridge when I saw him: A white man sound asleep on the bridge. There was a plastic bottle of water near one of his hands, as if he were reaching for it. The roof over the bridge kept him in shade. This, I reminded myself, was in a resort town. He was still there when I walked back after my stay in the medicinal hot springs, but the next morning when Elaine and I walked over the bridge to take the waters he was gone.

Story from Dr. Phillip K. Tompkins, St. Francis Center volunteer

A Day in the Clothing Room, Showers

From nine to ten I worked in the Clothing Room behind the counters with mainly men's clothing. The hour passed without any exceptional experiences except that Frank the Poet was not there to work with me handing out the desired clothing items. James stood in for him and I was eager to get back to the Men's Showers to hand out Joe Brzozowski's goodies. Joe is a St Francis Center volunteer for over 20 years. He buys smellgood out of his pocket. When I entered at 10:00 there was the usual guest also named Joe at the usual sink well into his 60 minute shampoo and combing routine. After noticing him I saw another man walking into the big room and over to the counter to ask me for shampoo, shaving cream and towels. He took the sink next to the perfectionist, and leaned over and began to soak his long, curly, thick black hair. What made him stand out for me—but apparently not the other guests who paid no attention—was the heavy, black overcoat he was wearing. He added shampoo and massaged his long hair over and over. After twenty minutes or so he began to shave, still wearing the overcoat on with the collar up. Joe was still combing his hair while standing next to him. The weather news later gave us a high of 94 for the day. I am afraid it would be impertinent if not an insult to ask the man: Why the overcoat on such a hot day?

A black man approached the counter and asked for soap. To prevent bars of soap from being used by more than one man, the shelter does not hand out a whole bar of soap to each person showering or washing in the sink. We break each bar into several chunks, each of which is big enough to clean a big, dirty man. I got the basket full of chunks and handed it toward him and realized the man had no fingers on either hand, only a thumb. I was not sure what to do but I decided to present the basket to him so that he could tell me which piece to select. Instead, he reached into the basket an picked up a white chunk by expertly pressing the chunk between his partial thumb and the side of his palm. He thanked me and moved toward the sinks.

And then came an old white man, carrying one of the baskets from the dressing area full of dirty, wet towels. He lifted the heavy basket up on to the counter. I have known him for many years and yet I do not know his name. Nonetheless we always fondly greet each other. It began maybe fifteen years ago when I would see his handsome face in the shelter and then again in the University Library on what is called the Auraria Campus in Denver near the building where we live. I was there to do research or check out a tome, while he would be reading a book at a table. We would smile and exchange greetings. This day I thanked him sincerely for saving me a trip into the dressing area to pick up a full basket that I would then take out my back door and on to the laundry. It was not the first time he has done this favor for me. He also asked me for an empty basket he could place back in the dressing area. I thanked him again and he smiled. I know few persons with the dignity and generosity of this nameless, homeless man who lives in a different, mysterious realm of existence.

Story from Dr. Phillip K. Tompkins, St. Francis Center volunteer

A Shift at St. Francis: Showers, Shampoo, Socks, a Towel… and perhaps a reason

The alarm was shrill and loud but it did its duty. I got to the shelter before 8:00 and got my schedule from Sara, the Coordinator for the day:

8:00 Men's Showers

9:00 Clothing Room Counter

10:00 Laundry

I walked in to relieve a volunteer named James in the showers. The place was in good shape and I praised James and he said that it had been busier earlier. The only problem: no clean socks. I groaned, knowing how important to men on their feet all day that they be able to trade in their dirty socks for a clean pair and slip them on after a hot shower. I hustled back to the laundry and found volunteers Pam and Frank at work folding washed towels. I told them of our need and they promised to get to work rolling some clean socks.

I went back to my lair and saw a bottle of shampoo on the corner where we keep our help-yourself-items. While hefting the large plastic bottle to estimate the amount of shampoo in it I heard a disembodied voice say "Towel." I decided that there was enough shampoo in the container and put it in its place on the towel in the corner. I turned to find the source of the request and saw a man with an angry demeanor turning to walk back to the dressing area. As I watched him I was hor-rified to see him reach into a basket of used towels and yank one out. Then he began to undress for a shower. I grabbed a clean towel, lifted the gate and walked toward the dressing area. When I reached him I handed him the towel.

"No," he barked and turned away, rejecting the towel and me.

I took the towel back to my shelf and picked up a basket of used towels to take back to the laundry. Pam and Frank had rolled enough clean socks to fill half of a large plastic basket. I thanked them and hustled back to the Showers to dispense.

Having lunch with my wife Elaine at the scene from the Showers came back to me. I told her about the man and the towel. I was trying to move beyond my sorrow and guilt and asked

"Do you think what he did might be part of why he is homeless?"

She smiled, took my left hand in her right one and held it.

Story from Dr. Phillip K. Tompkins, St. Francis Center volunteer

An Incident

Several of the employees were trying to do showers and towels. I went in the women's shower to get wet towels, and several women called to me as there was a woman on the floor. It's this lady that has recently come to SFC, and she looks 100 years old. She's very bent over, and she wears socks on her hands and smells strongly of urine. She had forgotten to get towels and was shivering. I went and got towels, wrapped her up and had her get up and sit in a chair. She wanted her old clothes back on. It took me about 30 minutes to coax her out of her sour smelling items, but I did. I washed a couple of things for her, and the water was black, and decided she just had to get new clothes. Sarah said it was ok. I wanted to take a picture of her when we were done. In her pretty purple and blues. I also took liberty to go through her plastic bags, threw out trash, combined all her cigarettes and got her a canvas bag for her belongings. She was very pleased with my kindness, and I felt God put me there at that moment as he knew I'd help her gladly and lovingly. We were quiet in mail from 10 to 11, so I cleaned drawers and cabinets.

Story from Joan Maybury, St. Francis Center volunteer

A Special Day

When I got back into the showers I saw and heard one of those moments that grabs me, makes me wonder what more we can do. A tall white man with short hair asked me rather timidly for something, perhaps Q,-Tips. He stood next to the counter and looked about the room. Someone who knew him called him by name and then asked him how he was doing.

"I'm OK," he said in that soft-spoken way.

"What are you gonna do today?"

"Oh, I don't know. "Today is my birthday."

"Happy Birthday to you, Happy Birthday to You . . . ." sang his friend. I joined in for a couple of lines.

At nine I moved into the clothing room, behind the counter where we keep the men's pants, tee shirts, underwear, and socks. I told Frank and Pat, working at the door, and they stopped when I got to the punch line. " Punch" in the sense of producing a jolt, not a laugh.

Story from Dr. Phillip K. Tompkins, St. Francis Center volunteer

Politics in the Shower

A handsome gray haired man came in, showered, then bought a razor to work on perhaps a week of growth. After shaving one sideburn he turned to look in my direction and began what became an unorthodox oration.

"You know Attorney General Barr?" I nodded and he continued.

"He is going to subpoena all those people, Democrats, for spying on Trump during the 2016 election." He went on to say that we should listen to Mark Levin and Sean Hannity on a radio station number I missed. He went on to say that Democrats had been letting in 500 people a day in Florida.

"Why?" I asked.

"To get their votes."

He said that Hillary personally "smashed" her emails.

I wondered if this political oratory, delivered with a pleasant smile, might become a problem. Looking around I found that only one other person had listened steadily—Phil Tompkins.

Story from Dr. Phillip K. Tompkins, St. Francis Center volunteer

Orphans

From ten to eleven I worked in the Laundry, spending most of my time trying to make matches of our freshly laundered socks. When we give used but clean socks to the men in the Showers, they put their dirty ones in a bucket with a detergent in it. We launder them in large batches and then have to match them. It always amazing when I wind up with a basket or two that cannot be matched. Wait, I just thought of something. What if there are a half-dozen socks in each batch washed that are "orphans," as Frank calls them. If they are saved and then get the other half dozen from the next wash, voila, we are building up a a whole basket of rejects that we should not waste time on trying to match. I will try to sell this hypothesis to others at the shelter and report back in a Story from the Shelter.

Story from Dr. Phillip K. Tompkins, St. Francis Center volunteer

"It was a truly beautiful
day this morning !"

It was a truly beautiful day this morning, sunny and warm as I drove to the St. Francis Center. But when I got to the shelter at 2323 Curtis I saw two police cars and an ambulance by the front door. No one seemed to know what it was all about. One person said the vehicles were there for different reasons. I took over at the Men's Showers at 8:00 a.m. from a volunteer named James who had opened them at 7:00. The number of men in the facility was about average and quiet. Until.

All of a sudden I could hear a half dozen loud voices talking about something I could not make out. I looked up at the area with sinks and mirrors and beyond it to the dressing area. There were five, maybe six tall black men speaking and listening intently about something. Then I heard the name Magic Johnson. Then another man said "LeBron," and I knew it must be about basketball. Of course, the NBA Finals are now underway. I looked again at the men and realized that every one of them must have been 6' 4" or taller. Perhaps they are former basketball players themselves.

Story from Dr. Phillip K. Tompkins, St. Francis Center volunteer

"It was good for both of us."

I did not feel great when I woke up at 6:15 before my alarm went off, but I thought I could prevail on my colleagues, other volunteers to help. My recent pattern is to start out at 8:00 a.m. in the Showers, then move to the Clothing Room at 9:00 and then either to the Laundry at 10:00 or back to the showers.

My legs were a bit shaky when I picked up my work slip and, sure enough, I was scheduled for the Showers at 8:00 and again at 10:00. What I worried about was the long trips carrying baskets of wet and heavy towels from the dressing area, back behind my counter, out the door into the Clothing Room, and then on to the laundry where I dumped them and carried lighter, clean, and dry towels back to the Showers.

I relieved James at 8:00 and he asked about my health, knowing that I missed volunteering the week before.

"I'm better but I am still worried about carrying those wet towels back to the . . . .:

"Ok," he interrupted, "Let me carry the dirty ones back right now and bring a lot of clean towels. If you do have to carry some dirty towels just put them outside the door. I will be back to carry them to the Laundry."

Relieved, I began one of the busiest periods ever in the showers. I did have to put a couple of baskets outside my door. Then an old, tired looking man came up to the counter with a towel around him and softly said:

"What am I going to do for pants?"

"Where are your pants?"

He paused and said softly:

"They had alcohol on them."

He walked back to the bench where his other clothes were. Some time later he came back to the counter wearing a fall sweater. When he moved the door I could see that he had a large towel wrapped around his waist, making a kind of skirt.

Looking at the door opening out to the main room with hundreds of people he spoke so softly that I could barely hear him ask

"Go out there wearing a towel?"

A younger man entering the door stopped and asked him

"Do you need a pair of pants? I have an extra pair," showing the clothes bag he was carrying, "size 34."

They walked away to the dressing area. Then the older man later appeared with a smile, his sweater, and a pair of khaki pants that fit him to a tee.

Later, after he had taken a shower, the younger man walked toward the exit with a smile.

"Thanks," I said, "That was a good thing you did."

"It was good for both of us."

And good for me I thought. I was having a spiritual experience, glad that I had come to work.

Story from Dr. Phillip K. Tompkins, St. Francis Center volunteer

It's good to give—and to smellgood

On Thursday after lunch I stopped at my barber shop, Stan's Downtown, on 16th Street just a block from our loft. When I walked in his lovely receptionist said

"Dr. Phil, we were just talking about you."

"I hope it was something good."

"Yes, it was. And Stan has something for you, some smellgood for the shelter." Stan walked in and also hailed me as "Dr. Phil. Let me go get the smellgood." He came back with a one gallon jug full of a light blue liquid. He handed it to me and I took a look at it. "After Shave" was printed on the label.

"Thanks, I'll take it to the St. Francis Center tomorrow. Smiles all around the shop.

I got to the shelter at about 7:50 on Friday and checked my work slip.

8:00 Showers

9:00 CR Counter

10:00 Laundry

I took it with me to the showers. We put small plastic cups on the counter for the men to use for mouthwash and other toiletries so I put an upside down stack of them next to the gallon to see if they would help

I got busy with the requests for towels, wash clothes, floor towels, soap, shampoo, and other items. A man asked for after shave so I referred him to the bottle. He liked the smell and put the contents of the cup into his palm and seemed to be pleased with it. I moved it over to the side of the counter where the men come in and go out of the shower room. I had to get some dirty towels out of the dressing area and when I came back I saw a man standing by the gallon bottle.

"This is as good as Aqua Velva," he said, slapping both cheeks.. . . . .

I talked my wife Elaine into an early lunch at the Rock Bottom, near Stan's Shop. He was delighted when I quoted the man about the comparison to Aqua Velva. "Well, it's not that good. But if he liked it, that's what counts."

He gave me a good, close cut and talked about giving. He felt bad for people who did not know how good it is to give. I forgot to ask how he knew about our shelter's need for smell-good. It is good that so many people I know enjoy giving to the St. Francis Center.

Story from Phillip K. Tompkins, St. Francis Center volunteer

"Brother, can you spare a -- razor?"

Not long after I moved behind the counter in the showers at 8:00 a.m., the young man I describe in another story as walking up to the counter and saying "Phil, I'm exhausted," walked up again and this time said

"Phil, I need a razor. But I don't have a dime."

I hesitated until tall middle-aged white man standing a few feet away said quietly, as if it were between just the two of them,

"Come on back with me and I'll give you a razor.

I had hesitated because I would have had to make a decision. Tooth brushes and razors are a dime each, combs or hair picks are a nickel. If a guest has no money I have learned that I have several options. One is to tell the guest that they could go up front and talk to one of the staff greeters on either sides of the entryway into the large room of the shelter. They can give a free razor, toothbrush, and comb to a guest once a month. Second, sometimes a fellow guest will come up with a dime or nickel to help a fellow guest. Occasionally a guest will give me a dollar bill for a razor, toothbrush, and comb, telling me to "keep the change and buy somebody else what they need." If that offer had not come up I might well have given him the razor on the basis of earlier donors.

It is heartwarming to see these acts of kindness to those who are completely down and need such an act to get on with the basics in life.

Story from Dr. Phillip K. Tompkins, St. Francis Center volunteer

Friday before Labor Day
at St. Francis Center

My work slip this morning of the last Friday of the month:

8:00-9:00 Showers

9:00-10:00 CR Counter

10:00-11:00 Showers

11:00-1145 Volunteer Meeting

I had not known about the meeting so I made a mental note to call Laini, my wife of 48 years, to tell her I would be home a bit later than usual. I relieved James in the Men's Showers so he could work in Mail and Storage. My work slip is full of scratch notes I made during the first and third hours in the showers. The tall young man who comes in with a heavy coat and thick stocking cap covering his ears and forehead did so today, the next to last day of August. He stands and watches the men in the showers but never speaks, never takes a shower. It was fairly quiet until 8:27 when we got a rush of guests, all asking for towels, soap, shampoo, lotion, socks, and "smellgood."

"Phil, you are hip," said the tall African American man with a smile after he asked for razor and a comb and I offered him a "pick." I smiled, taking it as a compliment. Another African American man stood by the counter to socialize with me between the requests from the men and my responses. Before he left he said "You're a good guy, Phil." I told him thanks.

Another man walked out saying "God bless you." Despite all their concerns about the next meal and the next night, many express their appreciation to the volunteers here to help.

A late middle-aged man asked me to keep his cane behind the counter until he finished cleaning up. I looked around the room and saw several older men, more than usual. Are we getting more older homeless people?

"Hey, it's my birthday" announced a guest in his early thirties, smiling as he said it. A friend countered with "Happy Birthday on Labor Day weekend."

"And the Taste of Colorado," he answered, referring to the many restaurants of Denver and suburbs who offer their favorite dishes from tents in the Civic Center.

A young, slender, tall white man no older than late teens or early twenties took a chair near the counter where he could watch me and talk to me behind the counter. He first asked for three towels, a floor mat, big towel, and wash cloth. Plus soap, shampoo, and conditioner. After he showered he asked for lotion, then sat in the same chair and lathered himself and watched me.

Nine o'clock came quickly. I was relieved by a staff member and went out of my back door into the Clothing Room, then behind the counter to work with Frank. I complimented Frank on his close haircut on the sides and back, making his baldness n top less striking. He complained that it was closer than he wanted, but I tried to reassure him it made him look better. He has a new walker now, one with all four legs. I offered him a CD by the Eagles that I thought I had borrowed from him, but he said he would borrow it from me and bring it back next week along with the first book on the Space Program I wrote. I agreed.

Then appearing at our counter was the young man from the showers who had sat where he could watch and talk to me. He looked different, his full head of hair looked less plastered than before his shower. He had picked out a pair of shorts from a box on one counter. Now he wanted everything to go with it. Underwear, tee shirt, socks, examining several samples carefully before making his choices. Again the time passed quickly with guests grateful—until we ran out of underwear. All underwear for men—except extra-large. A couple of average sized men took extra-large boxers because "I have to have underwear."

Back I went to the showers at 10:00: there he was back at the same chair, putting on the new clothes with great care.

"You seem to be getting ready for something," I observed.

He nodded.

"What?"

"Skating," he said.

"What?" I understood the word "skating" but thought I might be wrong.

"Skating."

"What kind? Roller skating?"

He shook his head, negative.

"Ice skating?" I asked incredulously.

"Skateboarding."

"Where?"

"At the rink."

"We have a board skating rink in Denver?"

"Yes."

"Where?"

He gave me the address but I forgot it because of my surprise. I had never heard of such a place, but now it seemed that all of his morning's preparations were to look good while skating for an audience of others. I decided to ask a basic question.

"Is it your life?"

"Yes," he said immediately, nodding his head and adding "It is my hobby."

Story from Dr. Phillip K. Tompkins, St. Francis Center volunteer

'Smellbetter' and 8 Razors

The first Friday of the year, January 3, 2020, was rather uneventful. The men in the showers seemed more relaxed now that the Christmas and New Year holidays had passed.

A large middle-aged black man said

"Give me some of that 'smellbetter' and I will be happy."

Never in my 21 years of working in the Men's Showers have I heard it called that. The code name for after shave and spray cologne, important morale boosters, is one word: "smellgood." Perhaps he misremembered or then he may have been trying to be original in the New Year. I made him smell better if not good.

Then a tall, muscular white man, maybe six four, handed me a dollar bill with a serious look on his face.

"I am giving you a dollar and I want only two razors at ten cents each. That leaves you enough to give eight razors to men who have no money." I nodded and gave him back two safety razors and another nod of appreciation.

At nine o'clock I moved on to the Clothing Room and stood behind the counter, again in the role of something of a bartender. The same tall white man walked up to receive service as I quietly announced him as

"The man who bought two razors for a dollar, leaving eight paid razors for those men who do not have any money."

He made several small bows and announced:

"I may need one of those razors myself."

Story by Dr. Philip K. Tompkins, St. Francis Center Volunteer

Joe Mendoza, 1949-1999

The headline of the September 2000 issue of Denver *Voice*, our local newspaper advocating for homeless people was "The Voice remembers." The story listed eight names of homeless men murdered in Denver in the preceding months. They were mistaken--only seven homeless men had been murdered in that time frame.

One name on the list stood out: "Joe Mendoza 1949-1999."

I knew Joe the best of the seven men murdered in 1999. He had been a boxing champion based in Los Angeles who worked out with movie stars. He was still handsome, well built for a man who drifted into Denver on a river of alcohol. As we learned of the seven murders, one at a time, we cringed and prayed. A police investigator told the media that they were going to treat the killings as a "crime." Mayor Wellington Webb answered those who asked why? He said they were "human beings."

One of the most brilliant men I ever knew, Kenneth Burke, wrote an essay about the concept of "Degrees of Being." A plant has more degrees of being than a rock. A human being has more degrees of being than a plant or a dog. Burke did not mention this possibility but I wrote that some human beings treat others as if they had fewer degrees of being.

Imagine how the homeless people felt about learning that one by one their peers were being beaten to death in Denver. Those of us serving them at shelters felt the same way. Joe

Mendoza knew me well enough to seek me out for a conversation about his experience of homelessness. He said he was sleeping in what was then an open field near the Union Station. Something woke him up and he saw a young Hispanic male standing between him and an "old wino." Joe said he made a fist and the young man apologized for disturbing him.

"But what was he doing there, Phil?

I told Joe that I did not know and had to get back to work. I thought about it all week and decided that on the next Friday I would draw Joe Mendoza aside and tell him to report what he saw and heard to the police. But I did not see Joe all day. At our prayer meeting at the end of our work the St. Francis Center Director, Tom Luehrs, said that the name of the latest victim beaten to death was "Joe Mendoza." I told Tom what had been said between the two of us and he said I should pass this information along to the police.

I did that and filled out a long report. Then I had telephone interviews in which a police investigator told me that although the media had reported that some of the men had been decapitated, they did not know that they had been beaten so thoroughly that their heads had melted into the ground. That is why their heads were not found. One of the cases was solved, but it was not the modus operandi used in most of the cases.

During the period in which the murders were taking place I was in the Men's Showers on a day when we got word that a fifth homeless man had been beaten to death. I was alarmed when an argument broke out between a showered and dressed black man and a white man in the showers speaking a language nobody else understood. Then another white, stocky man started shouting; a tall naked black man shaving his face and head at a sink responded but I could not understand. I started to call for help from staff members because I could see a racial battle between two groups of homeless men developing. I hesitated and then shouted for them to "cool it." The two dyads had squared off but the muscular white man said "We shouldn't even be doing this because of the murderer out there." The black man said something I could not hear but could see that he extended his hand toward the other. The white man took it and said "Yeah, man, we have to stick together." The image of the two naked men shaking hands is still with me, a memory of what we can do in the face of further trauma.

And the name Joe Mendoza is still with me. The men murdered in 1999 were not nameless, just homeless.

Story by Dr. Phillip K. Tompkins, St. Francis Center volunteer

THE SOJOURNER

I almost didn't see him sitting there
among the overgrowth in the alley,
this stranger with his back pack.
He nodded to me as I drove by,
and I quickly pulled into our garage
and lowered the door. Not alarmed,

but uneasy, as when something appears
out of place, I tell my husband,
and he goes to ask if he needs help.
"Just passing through," he says.

Maybe had the ancient laws
of hospitality been passed down
unbroken, we would have invited him
to join us for a cold drink, some food,

offered him our guest room,
this stranger, traveling in a foreign land.
He could even have been a god,
disguised in shabby clothing.

But all we will ever know is that
he was---"Just passing through."

Jane Costain
2019

"The Sojourner" first appeared in *Dash Literary Journal*

A birthday card, a sympathy card

This is a very personal expression of feelings about homeless persons, volunteering, St. Francis Center; and acknowledgment of a birthday and a death, by Dr. Phillip Tompkins, 20 plus year volunteer at St. Francis Center; author of a book on homelessness; and noted speaker on this subject. Dr. Tompkins supplied most of the stories for this book, and was a catalyst for its production. It seems a fitting way to close these Stories from the Shelter.

Gary Moore

This is a formal card with two purposes today, not a Friday Letter from the showers. Tuesday, October 8 was my birthday. My wife Elaine took me on the train to Glenwood Springs and back for my present. While there I bathed in the hot springs that Native Americans and many others think of as having healing powers. It is also my birthday month at the St. Francis Center.

I relieved James the smiling volunteer in the men's showers at 8:00. Denver had a severe drop in temperature Wednesday night after we returned home on the train. It surprised me by being a surprisingly uneventful morning in the showers. At nine o'clock I moved over to the Clothing Room and there we could see the effect of the colder weather. Many guests asked for gloves and "long johns," or long underwear. We had to say no because we had not put them out yet. Although no one gave us a reason, we did know from past seasons that if we give out winter clothes too early, our guests often take them off on warm days and forget them.

I did another session in the showers at 10:00. It was not terribly busy but hard to do my job because we ran out of clean socks we usually give out in exchange for a dirty pair. When relieved I walked back to the laundry to see friends among the volunteers. Joan Maybury was back from a vacation and working hard. Joe Brzozowski and I talked about our recent trips and then Tom Luehrs, the Director of SFC, approached us. Joe talked about his recent trip to the mountains with his wife June. I mentioned that while Elaine and I were in Glenwood Springs I read a long, well-written letter to the editor of the local newspaper. It took notice of the camps of homeless people in their tourist town and how harmful they could be. The writer urged readers to do something to break up the camps but said nothing about trying to help the people in the camps. Joe and Tom understood the problem

Then Tom came out with the bad news:

"Carla Slatt-Burns passed away yesterday."

Joe didn't remember her at first so Tom explained that she had worked for 22 years on the shelter's staff before retiring in 2018."

"She trained me to be a volunteer back in October 1998," I said.

Joe nodded and we chatted about how Joe and I had begun volunteering back in 1998, although he has a bit more seniority than I.

"Oh," I said, "I quoted her in a speech last Saturday at Trinity United Methodist Church. Deb Meyer, Director of Servant Ministries, organized a seminar on the effects of trauma on people we might have to serve at the church. I gave a twenty-minute speech about SFC and how seven homeless men had been murdered back in 1999." I also mentioned that when Carla Slatt-Burns trained me to be a volunteer she made an important point about communication: "Homelessness is not a noun, it is an adjective. It is *dehumanizing* to speak of 'the homeless' or 'a homeless.' They are homeless persons or humans.'"

Tom then projected the passing of a person from our era into our future:

"You two," nodding at Joe and me, "have to keep going for a while longer."

I hope we can, I said to myself, *because this is one of the most rewarding, if at times painful, most fulfilling experiences of my life.*

Birthday and sympathy cards by Dr. Phillip K. Tompkins, St. Francis Center volunteer.

A note about Practical Theology, St. Francis Center, and faith-- by Dr. Tompkins and Deb Meyer, Director of Servant Ministries, Trinity United Methodist Church, Denver.

I got to church early for our Sunday School Class at Trinity United Methodist Church; it meets from 9:30 to 10:30 and goes by the name of Trinity Academy. The ninety or so members tax ourselves to remunerate speakers, mainly professors of theology and divinity, to lecture us about topics of mutual interest.

The speaker for this Sunday, January 5, 2020, was Deb Meyer, with the intriguing title of Director of Servant Ministries for Trinity. She began by telling us of her background, born in that part of the Bible Belt known as Oklahoma to a religious family, and then moving back and forth and up and down the USA. She added that she had earned a Master of Divinity degree at Asbury Seminary in Orlando.

She then set out to stress the difference between the Greek division of Theoria and Praxis, or theory and practice. In her concern for the day, the theory in question was Theology, or what the scholar Kenneth Burke called "words about God." By citing sources from the theological right, for example, *Christianity Today*, a conservative or evangelical magazine, she submitted that there is push today to stress Practical Theology.

Hmm. When Elaine and I retired from teaching at the University of Colorado at Boulder and moved to Denver in 1998, we enrolled in a four-year course offered at St. John's Episcopal Cathedral called EFM, or Education for Ministry— the assumption that every Christian should have a ministry. The first year was the Old or Jewish Testament;

the second was the New Testament; the third year was given to Church History; the fourth year was given to Theoria or Theology. We both loved the fourth year but do not remember anything about Practical Theology.

What is Practical Theology? Meyer illustrated it in a couple of ways. The editor of the conservative magazine entitled *Christianity Today*, for example, recently broke with tradition by mentioning politics, by asking readers "to hold serious discussions about how our identity as Christians shapes our activity as citizens."

Meyer then identified Practical Theology by citing prophetic voices "that remind us that Jesus' public ministry was to fulfill the prophesy of Isaiah (63):
to proclaim good news for the poor
to proclaim freedom for the prisoners
to bind up the wounds of the brokenhearted
to heal the blind, and
to set the oppressed free."

We should care more, do more about deeds that enact the words, she seemed to be saying. Or, less emphasis on the words about God and more on the actions requested. Despite being a "word man," a professor and author, I readily accept that. Meyer in fact mentioned that "Phil Tompkins has been a regular volunteer at St. Francis Center for over 25 years."

Well, as indicated above, it is for over 21 years, from 1998 to 2020.

Meyer's talk sprinkled books and scholars on her audience: e.g., Joan Chittister's *A Call to Uncommon Courage*. She also turned to a founder of Trinity's larger church: John Wesley and his book *A Short History of the People Called Methodists*. She additionally cited *Good News for the Poor* by Theodore Jennings.

Meyer also provided an action step for her audience of Methodists who study theology: become a greeter, learning to greet new people to the church; help with the food served to poor at Trinity several times a week; volunteer for the shelter and other such organizations. The last lines: "And to make it easy, I offer my support coordinating at least one opportunity for you to serve together as a community this year—another way for you to develop relationships! You know where to find me."

I raised my hand to speak and stood to say:

" I want to compliment you for your remarks today. I was a volunteer at the St. Francis Center before I joined Trinity United Methodist Church. After joining I felt no sense of a common denominator, of commonality between the two organizations. Now you come along with Practical

Theology uniting us, making a common bond between the two."

I quit there because the audience had begun cheering and applauding before I finished. After a few days I sent Deb Meyer a copy of this letter to ask her if it captured the essence or spirit of her talk. She sent this reply:

I think you captured the essence of my perspective that the equilibrium between theology and praxis is righting, that the Christ-like is more than studying God. . . . to be like Christ requires that we put our understandings into action, going in faith to the people and places [where] we're not so comfortable. Blessings,
    Deb Meyer

This note by Dr. Phillip K. Tompkins

More about St. Francis Center and Trinity United Methodist Church

Trinity United Methodist Church is a long time supporter of St. Francis Center. Support includes extensive, organized volunteers and financial support through the Trinity Second Century Foundation. In the past, the Church transferred its *Turnabout* program to St. Francis Center, which now continues to support ex-felons with jobs and other services. This is done from the former home of Warren Methodist Church on Gilpin Street in Denver.

St. Francis Center moves forward

When I was relieved by a staff member I hustled into the meeting room. I then took a seat at the large round table. The chairs around it were soon filled by other volunteers. The Volunteer Coordinator had an agenda, the first part of which was about rules and procedures we volunteers have to voice. One for example, had to do with two guests getting into a fight. The policy is to stay out of it, to alert a staff member with more experience to take over.

Then Tom Luehrs walked in and took a seat. A large, handsome man, the Director of St. Francis Center had news for us: The City of Denver had given the St. Francis Center a grant of nearly a million dollars. The shelter will be modernized in many ways, perhaps the most important one is the expansion of the women's showers. We need many more of them and an attendant who can do the kinds of things for women that I do, passing out towels, toiletries, and handling the used towels. One of the facts that staggered me was part of the rationale for this expansion. Tom told us that in the "past seven years the number of women coming in as guests of the shelter had quadrupled from approximately 600 in 2012 to over 2500 in 2018.

The other news Tom had for us is that St. Francis Center had acquired Warren United Methodist Church that had been closed for lack of membership.

The St. Francis Center will create within it twenty SROs, or single-room occupancies. These would be used to house homeless people at St Francis Center ready for transition to assisted housing. These are wonderful improvements, but I had to observe to the group that "a fourfold increase in the number of homeless women visiting our shelter" was economically inconsistent with the fact that the U.S. economy had been moving toward the lowest unemployment percentage in recorded history.

Nevertheless, with these two announcements, St. Francis Center has positive momentum to move forward and continue to serve Denver's homeless men and women.

Story from Dr. Phillip K. Tompkins, St. Francis Center volunteer

About the Author / Story Collector

Dr. Phillip K. Tompkins

20+ year Friday volunteer at St. Francis Center

Dr. Phillip K. Tompkins is Professor Emeritus of Communication and Comparative Literature at the University of Colorado, Boulder. He is the author of a number of books including *Apollo, Challenger, Columbia: The Decline of the Space Program;* and *Who is My Neighbor: Communicating and Organizing to end Homelessness.*

His most recent book is *Managing Risk and Complexity through Open Communication and Teamwork,* published in 2015 by the Purdue University Press.

He is the Past president and Fellow of the International Communication Association and won the Peacemaker Award from the Rocky Mountain Conference of the United Methodist Church in 2016.

Dr. Tompkins has volunteered on Fridays for over 20 years at St. Francis Center Day Shelter in Denver. He is also a long time member of the Trinity United Methodist Church in Denver.

Gary T. Moore

Book compiler, editor, arranger

Gary Moore is a long time member of Trinity United Methodist Church in Denver. He was introduced to St. Francis Center, Dr. Phillip Tompkins and his stories by Deb Meyer, Director of Servant Ministries at Trinity, and through

Gary's volunteer work as President of the Board of the Trinity Second Century Foundation. This Foundation provides grants to Denver area nonprofits serving the Denver community. St. Francis Center has for several years been one recipient of these grants.